Dominie
Chapter
Books

Mailman Mario
& His Boris-Busters

By John Parker
Illustrated by E. Silas Smith

DOMINIE PRESS
Pearson Learning Group

Published by Dominie Press, an imprint of Pearson Learning Group, a division of Pearson Education, Inc., 299 Jefferson Road, Parsippany, NJ 07054.

DOMINIE PRESS

Pearson Learning Group

ISBN 0-7685-0317-5

Printed in Singapore

3 4 5 6   09 08 07 06 05

TABLE OF CONTENTS

Chapter One

A Mailman's Worst Nightmare

Mailman Mario was the best mail carrier in the little town of Pleasantville. His uniform was always clean and pressed. His bicycle was always polished. He always put the letters in the right mailboxes. And rain, hail, or shine, he always delivered the mail on time.

Everyone looked forward to seeing mailman Mario, because he always had a smile on his face. He'd stop and talk with people.

He patted the dogs and stroked the cats on his
mail route. He whistled to the birds. Mailman Mario
liked everyone, and everyone liked mailman Mario.

Then one day, a dog named Boris moved into the
neighborhood. Boris wasn't big–he was huge! He
looked more like a horse than a dog.

His teeth were long, sharp, and white. Boris slobbered when he looked at people, as if he were deciding which part of them he was going to eat first.

9

Boris also had a bark as loud as thunder. When he
opened his mouth and "WOOFED!" it sounded like
a mountain falling over. The cats arched their backs
and hissed. The other dogs ran off with their tails
between their legs. The birds rose like clouds from
the trees.

Mailman Mario got a terrible shock when he saw Boris for the first time. Just imagine! One moment Mario was happily delivering letters–one for Mrs. Johnson, three for Mr. Lee, two for Miss Lopez. He was smiling at everyone, patting the dogs, stroking the cats, and whistling to the birds. But the next moment...

Mario turned a corner on his bicycle and suddenly saw an enormous dog! It was so big that its front paws were leaning on the top of the tall fence in the front yard. In an instant, Mario saw the name *Boris* on the dog's collar. Then Boris barked twice. The first bark blew Mario's cap off. The second bark blew the letters out of Mario's hand.

Mailman Mario looked up at Boris in horror. "Good Boris," he tried to say. But he only managed to say, "G-g-g-g-g-g-g-g." Mario sounded like a rusty faucet trying to spurt water. Boris bared his awesome teeth. Mario had seen teeth like that before, but only in movies about sharks. Then Boris slobbered.

Mario jumped onto his bicycle and rode off as fast as he could. Letters spilled out of his mailbag and flew everywhere. Behind him, Boris barked again, and then jumped over the fence in one great leap. He galloped toward Mario and his bicycle.

"I'm going to end my days as a dog's dinner," Mario said to himself.

In two seconds, Boris reached Mario, but he didn't bite him. Instead, he wrapped his fangs around the back tire of his bicycle.

CHOMP!

His teeth bit deep as Boris closed his eyes in bliss.

PSSSST!

The tire hissed until it was as flat as an ironing board. Boris chewed happily on bits of rubber.

Chapter Two
Mario Meets His Match

Mailman Mario had to push his bicycle all the way home. It was hard work. And Mario was upset. For the first time ever, he hadn't delivered all of his letters. So people like Mrs. Johnson, Mr. Lee, and Miss Lopez wouldn't be getting the mail they expected.

"I'll have to think of a Boris-buster," said Mario.

Before he went to bed, Mario fastened a big black horn onto the handlebars of his bicycle.

When he squeezed the horn, it sounded like a hundred angry ducks.

PAAAAAAAARP!!

"Watch out, Boris," said Mario. "Tomorrow it's my turn."

But big Boris wasn't afraid of a hundred angry ducks. The next day, when the horn went PAAAAAAAARP!! Boris leaped over the fence as if he hadn't heard anything. He chased Mario and his bicycle down the road. His terrible teeth bit into the back tire.

CHOMP! PSSSST!

And Mario had to push his bicycle back home again, without delivering all of his mail.

Before he went home to fix his dinner, Mario went to the butcher shop and bought the biggest, juiciest bone he could find. He made a box with a side flap and tied it to the back of his bicycle. A long lever ran from the box up to the handlebars.

"This is my bone-in-the-box Boris-buster," he said.

Mailman Mario was so sure it would work that he almost looked forward to seeing Boris again.

The next day, he saw Boris waiting for him. The dog's massive paws were resting on the fence. Boris slobbered. His eyes gleamed. His loud barks shook the branches of the trees.

"Now!" said Mario. And he pulled the lever. The flap on the box opened, and out fell the juicy bone. It bounced on the sidewalk and came to a stop. Boris jumped over the fence and ran to the bone.

"It's going to work!" Mario said happily.

But it didn't. In fact, Boris didn't even bother to sniff the bone. All he wanted was the back tire of Mario's bicycle.

CRUNCH! PSSSST!

Chunks of rubber flew into the air as Boris chomped into the tire like a hungry shark.

Once again, mailman Mario had to push his
bicycle all the way home.

Chapter Three

Try, Try Again

Before he sorted the mail the next day, Mario went to see his supervisor. He told her about Boris. He told her about the horn, and about the bone in the box. His supervisor took a boxing glove out of a cupboard. She handed it to Mario.

"Show that Boris who's boss!" she said. "Give him a punch in the nose!"

"But Boris is so big," said Mario. "I can barely *reach* his nose!"

The supervisor reached into another cupboard and pulled out a long metal arm with a red button at one end. She put the boxing glove on the other end and pointed it at the wall.

"Watch this, Mario," she said.

She pressed the red button.

WHOOOOMPH! The arm shot out faster than a cheetah!

CRUNCH! The boxing glove punched a hole in the wall.

"See?" said the supervisor.

Mario's eyes opened wide in wonder. He nodded his head. What a Boris-buster this was! He couldn't wait to use it.

But the next day, mailman Mario was nervous as he started delivering his mail and getting closer and closer to the house where Boris lived. His legs trembled. His hands shook. His bicycle wobbled. And he pressed the red button at the wrong time, when the metal arm was aimed at Mrs. Johnson's mailbox!

WHOOSH! The metal arm smashed into the mailbox, just as Mrs. Johnson was reaching for her mail. She yelled and fell backward into a rose bush when the metal arm raced past her nose.

The boxing glove came loose and flew through the air. It knocked off Miss Lopez's sun hat and landed in Mr. Lee's birdbath, just as Mr. Lee was filling it.

Mrs. Johnson, Miss Lopez, and Mr. Lee were not happy.

Boris was so excited by all of this that he barked louder than ever. And once again, he bit into Mario's back tire.

PSSSSSST!

So mailman Mario had to push his bicycle all the way home again. And for the fourth day in a row, Mario didn't deliver all of his letters.

Mario decided he wouldn't use the boxing glove again. It was too dangerous. Instead, he collected a pile of leaves and branches. Then he got a big pot of glue and a ball of string.

He worked all night on his new Boris-buster.

By morning, Mario's bicycle was an amazing sight! There were branches and leaves everywhere. There was a hole in the branches so that Mario could see where he was going. There was even a bird's nest on the bicycle. And a notice for Boris:

ATTENTION, BORIS
THIS IS A TREE.
SO DON'T BITE THE BACK TIRE!

ATTENTION, BORIS
THIS IS A TREE.
SO DON'T BITE THE BACK TIRE!

But ... it didn't work.

CRUNCH! Boris still bit the tire.

PSSSSST! The tire still went flat.

Then Boris, with bits of rubber in his mouth,
circled the bicycle. Finally, he went back into his yard.

Chapter Four
A Boris-Buster That Works!

When he got home, Mario didn't know what to do. The horn didn't work. The bone in the box didn't work. The boxing glove didn't work. And trying to pretend that the bicycle was a tree certainly didn't work. Boris always bit the back tire. He liked the taste of rubber, and he liked to rip it with his teeth.

Then mailman Mario had a brilliant idea. Because the tire was hollow, he could fill it with something Boris wouldn't like. Something that would make him gasp, make his eyes water, and make his tongue hang out. Something that would make him *never* want to bite a tire again.

Something like ... MUSTARD!

Mario rushed to the supermarket and bought a dozen jars of mustard.

Then he went back home and emptied all of the mustard into a bowl of water. He stirred and mixed it all into a yellow paste. It was so hot, it sizzled. It was so hot, Mario's face turned red!

Mailman Mario cut a small hole in his back tire
and poured in the mustard mixture. Then he opened
his bicycle repair kit and covered the hole with his
strongest patch.

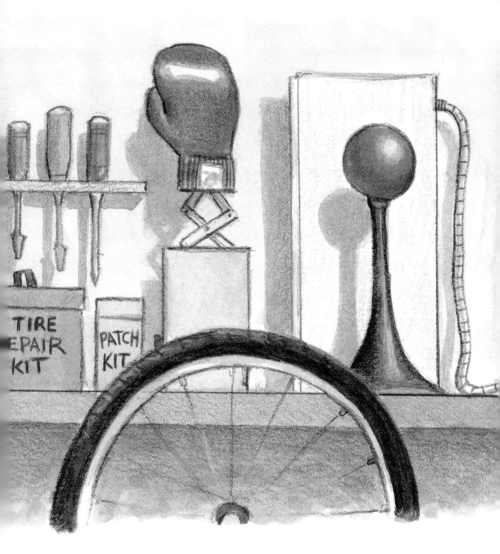

"I can't have any mustard leaking out," said Mario.
"I need it all."

When he was finished, he looked at the tire and
patted it.

"Are you my Boris-buster?" he asked.

Sure enough, the next day Boris bit into the tire. CHOMP! PSSSST!

But this time there was another noise. It didn't come from the tire. It came from Boris.

"YEEEEEAAAAAOOOOO!"

Boris opened his mouth wide, and his tongue flopped out. Tears streamed from his eyes. Steam came out of his ears.

Boris jumped back from the tire as if it were a rattlesnake! He bounded down the road and leaped into Mr. Lee's birdbath. He drank up all the water in three or four giant swallows. Then he opened his mouth wide so that Mr. Lee could squirt in even more water with his garden hose.

"At last," said mailman Mario. "A Boris-buster that works!"

Now, mailman Mario smiles at everyone again. He delivers all the letters at the right time and into the right mailboxes.

He whistles to the birds. He strokes the cats. And he pats the dogs.

Even Boris!